The Cities

THE CITIES

by Paul Blackburn

Grove Press, Inc., New York

for Frances Frost, her shade

Contents

AUTHOR'S NOTE

Well, here it is. And it turns out to be cities, or, I've held it to that. The Cities. Every man's stand be his own. Finally, it is a construct, out of my own isolations, eyes, ears, nose, and breath, my recognitions of those constructs not my own that I can live in. The Cities.

Of the poems, let me use Lorca's term: *duende* is that faculty of making/ into which you subsume yourself, your nickel, your dime, your cruzeiro, your peso, your five-dollar gold piece, your talent, silver mark, or denier, a goddamn ha'penny, if that's all you're carrying around in your pocket that day, you lay it on the line, it's payment, to whatever devil or demon wishes (with that idea or feeling IT feels itself itself, it's owner, if you like) to take possession of the THING in you, giving that quality to the process. The secret of this book is
three:
scissors, rock, and paper.

—PAUL BLACKBURN

Straight rye whiskey, 100 proof
you need a better friend?
Yes.   Myself.

The lights
the lights
the lonely   lovely   fucking   lights
and the bridge on a rainy Tuesday night
Blue/green double-stars   the line
that is the drive and on the dark alive
gleaming river
Xmas trees of tugs scream and struggle

                    Midnite

Drops on the train window wobble . stream
                    My trouble
                                    is
it is her fate to never learn to make
                    anything grow
                    be born or stay
Harbor beginnings and that other gleam . The train
is full of long/way/home and holding lovers whose
          flesh I would exchange for mine
          The rain, R.F.,

          sweeps the river as the bridges sweep
          Nemesis is thumping down the line
          But I have premises to keep
          & local stops before I sleep
          & local stops before I sleep

The cree-
ping train
joggles
rocks across
I hear
the waves below lap against the piles, a pier
from which ships go
to Mexico

a sign which reads

PACE O MIO DIO

    oil

"The flowers died when you went away"

Manhattan Bridge
a bridge between
we state, one life and the next, we state
is better so
is no
    backwater, flows
        between us is
our span our bridge our
naked eyes
open here
see
bridging whatever impossibility. . . PACE!

PACE O MIO DIO

    oil

"The flowers died . . ."
Of course they did

14

Not that I was a green thing in the house

        I was once.
        No matter.

The clatter of cars over the span, the track
                the spur
the rusty dead/pan ends of space
    of grease

We enter the tunnel.

The dirty window gives me back my face

From the first shock of leaves their alliance
with love, how is it?

Pages we write and tear
Someone in a swagger coat sits and waits on a hill

It is not spring, may-
be it is never spring
maybe it is the hurt end of summer
the first tender autumn air
fall's first cool rain over the park
and these people walking thru it

The girl thinking:
     life is these pronouns
the man : to ask / to respond / to accept
     bird-life . reindeer-death
     Life is all verbs, vowels and verbs
They both get wet

     If it is love, it is to make
     love, or let be
     'To create the situation / is love
        and to avoid it, this is also
     Love'
as any care or awareness, any
other awareness might might

     have been
     but is now

hot flesh
socking it into hot flesh
until reindeer-life   /   bird-death

You are running, see?
you are running down slope across this field
I am running too
to catch you round

        This rain is yours
        it falls on us
        we fall on one another

Belong to the moon
we do not see

        It is wet and cool
        bruises our skin
        might have been
        care and avoidance
        but we run   .   run

to prepare
love later

for Fee

Man
sits in a rattan chair
staring away to not care, to
wear nothing
get no haircut, to not
see the table behind him
filled with empty glasses
wine bottles

In the eye of his mind, the table
bare . the bottles
of rare wines
all empty

to write poems, say,
is not a personal achievement
that bewilderment

On the way to work
two white butterflies
& clover along the walks

to ask   .
to want that much of it   .

The little lights in the alley
great arclights on the bridges
     and the edges of parks.

               The young
are beautiful, walking past in the dark, in the
night, couples, two pairs, three,
children alone   .   Children   .

        They've a different world than we had,
              more brilliant, darker   .
        Hip or unhip, there's the same thing
        that edge of warm light ahead of them.
        Darkness they know   .   yes, they
        know the isolations   .   come .

Some,
fearing the example of their parents, are
afraid to love   .   others fearing
the example of their parents,

are helpless before the emotion, not
believing it possible.

        "I'm 16 years old," says one girl, "and
        never been kissed.
        "But I make it once in a while."

The generation,
or two if you like, ahead of them
uses deodorants.
        They, tho,

like the smell of hot flesh
suffering relief of its passion.

Sloppy and full of bravado they will live beyond us.
Their cocks dripping helplessly
their cunts full of sperm.

Two classes of Hunter High School girls
came to a recommended M. D.
to be fitted for diaphragms, ac-
(knowledged
companied by their mothers.
The M.D. felt better about her son
who dated sometimes
girls from Hunter HS.

Little lamps in the alley
streetlights in Brooklyn
like any midwestern town:
protect the young from their elders
while,
a lo mejor, they fuck
close, or at worst go down on each other
business of hands for the tender
touch at least
they
the night

Great arclights at the edges of parks
along bridges, Manhattan to Brooklyn
or the other way
(Where are you?
The sodium flares
make public

the new world rising
from the dark waters

from dark grass.

Pink and blue.
The pink striations angle down the sky
enter the southern deeps,   keep
laying out across my eye
asleep where it may not lie down
                    tell lies truly
        and see
love's breasts at attention, at rest, at
        my hand, orange
                sand,   this
        sunset you also see
but with two islands between you and me—

And if the sun is down
                our hearts
        the lights, the darks
they still are up, are high o
dance with me
        O,
                dance
                    with me   !

Here, in late spring, the summer is on us already
               Clouds and sun,
                  a haze over the city.   Outside my
window the ailanthus nods sleepily under
                  a hot wind, under
                  wetness in the air, the brightness
of day even with overcast.   The chair on the next roof
                  sits by itself and waits
for someone to come stretch his length in it.   Suddenly

thunder cracks to the south over the ocean, one can
                  shuteye see
the waves' grey wife, the storm, implacably stride
rain nipplings on the surface of the sea, the waves
                  powerfully starting to rise, raise their
                  powers before the hot wind
The endless stretchout to Europe disappears, the
rainsweep moving toward the city rising caught in the haze-
                  hot island atmosphere
      Hate anger powers whip toward the towers rising
from the hum of slugbedded traffic clogging avenues, the
                              trees
                  of heaven gracing their backyards crazily
                  waving under the strengthening wind

                  sun brighter
                  more thunder
                  birdsong
                  rises shrilly announcing the
storm in advance in encroach in abstruse syllables of pure
     SOUND   .   SONG   .   SOMEONE

comes to the porched roof to cover the chair from the
                    thunderfilled wet atmosphere,   there is
nothing clearly defined wrong I can see except
I must go uptown and see what other storms there
                    be, there

And paint the inside of my wife's white filing cabinet red
that all things may be resolved   correct   and dead   .

The fly on the floor
of the Unemployment Office
                              in Carlisle Street, walks
in quick little spurts as though on wheels, going
            nowhere, circling, tribbling about
            in a circle   :   when, lash, I
            dash my foot out at him, he
flies a few inches away and lands
                              crouched
                              sluggish
            then circles back toward my foot
where it stands in line with other unemployed feet

Poor fly,
March is too early in springtime for you to buzz our heads,
black speck on brown tile floor, you
are probably also
trying to get in line.

for Joel

Nice day,
sweet October afternoon
Men walk the sun-shot avenues,
                              Second, Third, eyes
                              intent elsewhere
ears communing with transistors in shirt pockets
                    Bars are full, quiet,
discussion during commercials
                         only
Pirates lead New York 4-1, top of the 6th, 2
Yankees on base, 1 man out

What a nice day for all this— !
Handsome women, even
dreamy jailbait, walk
                    nearly neglected   :
men's eyes are blank
their thoughts are all in Pittsburgh

Last half of the 9th, the score tied 9-all,
Mazeroski leads off for the Pirates
The 2nd pitch he simply, sweetly
                              CRACK!
belts it clean over the left-field wall
Blocks of afternoon
acres of afternoon
Pennsylvania Turnpikes of afternoon   .   One
                    diamond stretches out in the sun
                              the 3rd base line

27

and what men come down
it

The final score, 10-9

Yanquis, come home

"It would be—
          a mercy if
you did not come see me . . .

"I have dif-fi / culty
          speak-ing, I
cannot count on it, I
am afraid it would be too em-
                ba
                rass-ing
for me   ."

          —Bill, can you still
            answer letters?

"No   .   my hands
are tongue-tied . You have . . . made

a record in my heart.
          Goodbye."

                              October 1962

O god.
First the greatest right-handed batter in history
Rogers Hornsby (hit .424 in 1924) with a lifetime
average of .358—
and now William Carlos Williams

January 5
March 4
1963

Who in New York in 1965 would have
such incredible taste as to do a little girl's hair
in long skinny skeins of curl *à la*
Shirley Temple, *Little Miss Marker* stage?

The wonderful Puerto Ricans. The
taste so bad, the effect is wondrous
beautiful, and so she is

a brown little waif-wife, 5-yr-old opposite me on a
Lexington Avenue train
in a peppermint red-&-white stripe dress with
some legend needlepointed neatly in across
the bottom of the skirt I can't read

       BELO   —TO—

                                   it says.
She pulls it down prim looking at me
reproaching?   Can it be?
                She thinks I'm looking up her dress?
So I do.
          Not very interesting.
It's her eyes that get me :   the
severe quality in the reproach
has already faded, re-
                      ceded in favor of
                           —migod— friendliness.
A friendly reproach, then, from *Shirle Temple,*
that's fading away, and there's a
look of satisfaction (5 yrs old?)
that makes me wonder what my face looks like.

The part of the skirt she'd tucked between her knees
pops up again—starch, crinoline maybe?
                    well, it's still not very interesting.
                    Her father finds something, tho, there's a spot
just above her right knee, bruise, dirt, what's
that? he asks, she shrugs, he takes his hand away.

The letters visible on the skirt read now:
                    —LONGS   —TO—
                    I guess the legend now, it's incredible, he
                    can't keep his hands off her legs, lays
                    his slender hand over her knee just as
                    they rise to exit at Grand Central
                    Station   . Well, I'm right, the skirt
does have a crinoline and the message reads finally:
                    MY HEART BELONGS TO DADDY

I ' l l j u s t b e t   .   The curls down
the back of her neck are perfect.   In
her care not to scuff the patent leather shoes
with their sad shine,
                              she stumbles a bit at the doors
Goodbye, *Shirle Temple,* goodbye   !

which close
all at once   .

Leer
and that spine moved
back against another   (not surprising)   extension
of time(?)less stone is time perceived.
Let
the bereaved laugh with remembrance : here
one hand cups the handsome uppermost breast,
the other, the cup itself! A feast is death!

Across a slab of centuries, the living
flesh need not doubt itself or what they meant.
The slow brown eye of time and the quick blue
eye of lust
have crossed the line, forgiven themselves, become
an ornament.

*"Things are different when you come
across them again: they seem to have
increased power to enter one's soul
more sadly, deeper still, more softly
than before, melting into that sort
of death that is gently accumulating
inside one, day by day, underhand-
edly, each day making you defend
yourself a little less than the day
before."*

—Louis-Ferdinand Celine

After many times,
and never having liked the town,
Paris is softer this time.

The 1st reservation indecently cancelled on us,
a fight with the *concierges* in a second hotel,
                we are now peacefully settled
                in the Place Dauphine en l'Isle,
                au plein con de Paris.

The sex of Paris.
40 trees in this square
opposite the very white Palais
                de Justice
                que n'existe pas. But

soft . . . but then,
we have seen it softer when it was an indifference.
                One can
understand the aura of a woman—without contact, not
                falling in love

34

but now?   September?   Rain?   o christ, Paris
                    tout à fait normal.

Window left open all afternoon
and a dozen leaves drifted in
feuilles des marroniers
                    dans cette place 40.
How the wind lifts them up!
                    Indifferent.   Wet leaves.

Our string of peppers hangs by the window.
The owner has a southern accent. Good
coffee in the tabac
on the corner,
with buttered bread for the mornings.

                    In passage
Paris is softer this time
—or we are, for once,
altho *la misere existe*
altho *elle est partout*
for once it is Rome, New York, Athens, Madrid, and
like them, unique, herself, not *just* capital. The

            one man I know who loved her
                            is gone

        Et puis, maintenant,
        c'est déjà l'automne . . .

on a des choses,
on a tellement des choses   .   *Et maintenant,*
                    la Paris,
                    cette vielle belle,
c'est à nous.

35

Les feuilles mortes drift in at the window.

C'est à nous,
c'est à nous.

for Jean Séguy

              THE   MIRACLE   HAS happened   .
Here, after long winter, to see
                    this man
          looking at his town,
walking thru the air of it,
tho the sun is still pale on the walls
but thru the air of spring
looking at the sun on the walls

        smelling it
        head high   .
Not a glance at the window of the bookstore
which has taken   5   minutes of his attention
each time he has passed it
                              all winter   .

                    Toulouse, March 1955

Un sirventes ai fach
Contra'l ciutat de Tolosa
On m'avia pretz ostalatge
D'un sen salvatge e famosa
Del mons . . .

PB / 1956

I have made a sirventes against the city of Toulouse
           and it cost me plenty garlic :
and if I have a brother, say, or a cousin, or a 2nd cousin,
I'll tell him to stay out too.
        As for me, Henri,

      I'd rather be in España
      pegging pernod thru a pajita
      or yagrelling a luk
      jedamput en Jugoslavije,
      jowels wide & yowels not
      permitted to emerge—
      or even
      in emergency
      slopping slivovitsa thru
      the brlog in the luk.
      I mean I'm not particular,
      but to be
      in the Midi

      now that rain is here,
      to be sitting in Toulouse
         for another year,

                    the slop tapping in the court
                    to stop typing just at ten
                        and the wet-rot setting in
                    and the price is always plus,
                        I mean, please,
                            must I?

Whole damn year teaching
trifles to these trout with trousers
tramping thru the damp
with gout up to my gut
taking all the guff, sweet
                        jesus crypt,
                        god of the he
brews, she blows, it bawls, & Boses
(by doze is stuffed)
by the balls of the livid saviour, lead be
back hindu eegypt-la-aad
before I'b canned for indisciblidnary reasons.

                    O god.
                    The hallowed halls
                    the ivy covered walls
                    the fishwife calls
                    & the rain falls

                        Basta!

Jove, god of tourists, the whores in Barcelona are beautiful,
you would understand.
Weren't there Europa and Io? and Aegina, twin sister of
                                            Thebe
both daughters of Asopus?

and Maia and Antiope and
Niobe of the Thebans.
Eagle, ant, bull, beaver, flame, otter, how *not*?
Remember Leda?
I swan, you never felt old.
Your shower of rain at least was a shower of gold.
A gentle white bull with dewlaps.
The bulls in Barcelona are beautiful, Jove,
need no persuasion, are themselves as brave.

My old Guillem, who once stole this town,
thinking your wife's name enuf reason to . . .

St. Julian, patron of travellers, *mi des mercey*!

        Who else invoke? Who else to save
        a damned poet impaled by a *beterave*?
Mercury! Post of Heaven, you old thief, deliver me
from this ravel-streeted, louse-ridden, down-river,
gutter-sniping, rent-gouging, hard-hearted,
            complacent provincial town,
where they have forgotten all that made this country the
belly of courage, the body of beauty, the hands of heresy,
the legs of the individual spirit, the heart of song!

        That mad Vidal would spit on it,
        that I as his maddened double
        do — too
        changed, too changed, o
        deranged master of song,
        master of the viol and the lute
        master of those sounds,
        I join you in public madness,
        in the street I piss
        on French politesse

that has wracked all passion from the sound of speech.
A leech that sucks the blood is less a lesion. Speech!
this imposed imposing imported courtliness,   that
the more you hear it the more it's meaningless
                          & without feeling.

              The peel is off the grape
              and there's not much left
              and what is left is soured
              if clean   :
              if I go off my beam, some
              small vengeance would be sweet,
              something definite and neat,
                    say total destruction.

Jove, father, cast your bolts
& down these bourgeois dolts   !

        Raise a wave, a glaive of light, Poseidon,
        inundate this fish bait   !

           Hermes, keep my song
           from the dull rhythms of rain.

              Apollo, hurl your darts,
              cleanse these abysmal farts
              out from this dripping cave
              in the name of Love.

When the track rises
the wires sink to the fields

Trees absorb them in and blot them out
black running
pencil-lines against the fields' green

Shrubbery close to the track goes by so
               fast it hurts the eyes

Rain has quit
We have arrived
at Salut or Castelnaudary

          A woman laughs harshly in the corridor
          The soldiers on either side sleep beautifully
peacefully, one with his mouth open, the
          other has his closed
          The world is certainly diverse!
                  Wires begin again to
                  fall and rise
          Small fruit trees stand in quadrangles
          in a field otherwise planted
          The brook tries to escape notice and where
                 shall I put 2
          cypresses,
          3 elms?

       Old woman in the corner
wrestles her rented pillows and cannot sleep
       One finally arranges itself
under her right arm, the other

entirely out of control, she clutches
on her lap, the comfortable weight,
her rented buffers against a hard world
and stares direct in front of her and cannot sleep

My wife holds her face up for a kiss
Brow puckered and tired, she also cannot
quite sleep,
worrying about a pair of sunglasses we
left at someone's house yesterday
                    in the round of farewells.

Having left that town
we have left nothing behind.

The world is surely diverse enough
and if the information is sound, one
could ride forever and never fall off
              let others sleep—
I am so wide-awake I want to sing, while
the wheels turn, the windows clatter, the door
              jogs, the wires
rise and change and fall
and the green grass grows all round, all round
and the green grass grows all round . . . . . .

Long sideburns & teeth showing,
the teeth showing, seedy boy,
      overcoat slack, he's back,
      that figure of joy
to offer the subway system & everyone on it

          this 1 A.M., of
          April 9, 1964
            seeds,

or what it / I / they / we /
needs   .

The jews burn wood on First Ave., New York City, in a
                    barrel, to keep
                        w a r m
Clayton's
workmen across the cut
their house in Kyoto, likewise
warming their hands, the same cans or barrels, in the dark
flames leaping, men standing around, and
I have seen it on the West Side, New York, Gansevoort
                                                    Street
growing up among the meat packers there, would go
                        out
           at night
                                    hunting wooden crates
break up for the fireplace
to keep   w a r m,   my
mother's hands those days,
warming her arthritic smile   .   hands
& I myself in that
furnished room on 15th Street that had a fireplace, I
knew where to go to score for crates
                                    /   Good
           king Wenceslas went out
                        gath-er-ing
           on St. Stephen's day
                        winter fee-yew-well, or
                        the vacant lot at Houston
                        between Mott & Third

the same barrels
& cans & older men in long

overcoats from the mission,
& here the scene unabated   /   20-odd years later
the fruit & vegetable market, First Avenue & Ninth, using
                    wood from crates
New Jersey, Delaware, Cali-

                              for-ni-yay,
Florida, New Mexico, Georgia, Louisiana, Texas, all
for the same fire, how
reunite the South and North, the West and East—

                              warm,
in sunlight you never see it, just
                              walking by &
feel the warmth   .   there   .
Fire in a barrel, burning
the hands, the hands, the italian
bakery next door is still discreet,
but the kosher butchershop next to
that comes out for a word or two, the
                    gesture,
          palms stiff out at arms' length, passing
the time of day, their magic h a n d s
liverspotted and reddened maybe, no *peios* or beard, still
                    here at First Avenue and Ninth Street, it's
               the jews uniting the world, the country, the city,
          mankind down geological time perhaps,
to keep their hands warm   .

End of September. At
19th Street and Fifth Avenue
on the sidewalk in front of
the U.S. Employment Service
a colored lady looks at her watch.
Five of nine.
She shines in the sun impatiently

In Madison Square Park
young Persephone from the Bronx
emerges from subway
ducks her head into
the *Daily Mirror,* walks
not hearing the message
in Puerto Rican Spanish
delivered toward her ear
by a passing young man from Third Avenue and 26th St.
Lady!
You're being flirted with—
enter your life!

I wonder,
does this fountain run all night?
The park smells like an autumn hayfield, dried
leaves, dried grass all heaped together to be
burned in hazy afternoons by men
          with rakes and visor caps.
Sparrow
looks at fountain ambitiously
and settles for puddle next to it, left
from last night's rain.

In another puddle nearby, a big one,
seventeen disreputable-looking pigeons splutter and
splash and duck their heads
                    and drink and gargle away.
                    Among them a single warbler
green and tan wings splayed
digs long beak into underbelly
                    makes his toilet.

It is settled in already
the birds all employed with their hygiene
the unemployed with their newspapers
on street corners or park benches
Persephone with her page 5
young Hermes off on his errand, hopeless
bums preening outside the public facilities,
and center of it all, this
fountain plashes away   .   And finally
                    today   .   there are
more leaves on the surface of the pool than dixie cups
                    Fall is come

I'm sorry
life was tranquil (sort of)
then

'when you but lifted the glove of one white hand'

etcetera

the heavy pressure
of the presence of your body in the room
moving
O love,
is the end of my
imaginings
this late afternoon
feeling again at this window
the sensation of weight received
in that displacement
the small waves
lapping against me
constantly

—You are wearing a very zen dress,
        he told her
                And she was, the silly Hungarian.
—A very *zin* dress? she asked
            —T h a t ' s   r i g h t, he said
            and put his hand there   .
—Vulgarian?
       —No   .   zenless in aiza
            guyless in aaza   .
Standing in the high cool rooms   .
Walking the corridors   .

                        SHE HOLDS HIS HAND

     ladra, el ladrido, it
     means barking
—yes, and
this warm spring night, the
dogs do, different dogs
my different voices . and
     the other sounds : a
man across the vacant lot
laying it down to his wife, the
drunk upstairs thinks he's silently   padding
across the floor in stocking feet, it thumps, it's
     Friday night

    "Don' bodderme nomore, yhear?"
    thumps
and the dogs
bark this re-
assuringly peaceful, warm, spring—

The phone rings, it brings a
friend at 6th & Ave. D, beyond
Tompkins Sq. Pk., the other
       side of town,
& behind the warm voice I hear

a radio on & hear
the dogs bark there

Small,
Polish they told him, bar, East Seventh Street
Saturday nights
is the only one still open after 2 A.M.
             hence
                        crowded   .   to so prowl
even crowded is cool and quiet :
the bowling machine in one corner keeps the score
         with little clicks, sighs, and bells, the
jukebox down the wall turned down from concert size
                        no blare   .   the bar
packed, tables in the back near empty   .

         Jukebox: Slav, Slovene, Russian, Polish, Hun-
         garian, all that lonely impassioned *schwarze
         zigeuner,* the violin catguts to tear the heart if
         it be torn already.

Whose is not?

                        ◈

Midsummer madness by the sea at night, *las
olas doblandose siempre*
knees dug into the cool sand
couples spread out between the
rocks hiding from the beams of
policecars patrolling boardwalk

he arranges the blanket properly
             properly
waves slosh among the rocks

53

One feels an intruder and walks
            away
            slowly back
toward the lights, the light surf repe-
titious, dull in the ear   .

                    The lovers will swim forever.
                    The whole night.

                              ◈

        Coming out of the bar, slosh, the waves, lovers
        sleep lightly, their hot life away for a while, their
        arms, coming out of the bar violins, gulls sleep
                              on the waves,
        cry at his back
        until the door closes   .   streets wet
                              the summer rain

Reflections more shimmering and real than
the lights, dull surf, than any wall
where the mind goes blank.

Two Songs

for Joel

1

Stay drunk!
that's my motto   .
Then you'll never have to know
if the girl love you or no
                    (hee hee hee
                    nor will she

2

Play gui-
tar, go to the bar
hope there's one hand will caress
and undress
But pints to go
before you sleep
                    (har, har,
                    nobody care

What is there sits anonymous

                  in the subway and
destroys our eye for
anything else for
hours?   It is today the eastern Mediter-
                 ranean, she
                 just sits there, dark-
complexioned, that
neat slight hook to nose, the
rosebud mouth of a persian princess, but al-
                 ready too full
                 upper and
lower and maybe the one, the fun, the great
whore of Port Saïd or Babylon who scholarly sits
there knowing the liner, the
shadow on perfectly, an-
other shadow swinging under the cheekbones as she
turns to note number or name
on the station, the neat hook, the persian
arabian, afghan, indian, pakistani, lebanese, eyes
black, black, egyptian, mesopotamian, mouth pale, pale

She gets out at 14th St. and Union
Square and speaks
to a strapping old Irishwoman about
the change of trains

A last glimpse,
the local pulls out slowly, too
slowly, she stands there,

legs parted under the black coat of fake fur, she
just stands there, endlessly, taking
neither express nor local, stands
there on the 14th Street platform
the whole eastern Mediterranean history between her
thighs

                                  thinking

        It is a
        goddamn
        fucking
        shame
        to let a woman
        (woman!)
        built as you are
            (built)
      go

and this some bright november day when wind whips dis-
carded   (so many)   afternoon   (birds)
newspapers   (about us
            swirl of
                gulls)   above
                the subway gratings

In port, laughing & drinking
        jocundus jovialis
            yesterday.

        Today, horizon
holding the ship lightly
        is a girdle.
            His eyes
        are its eyes
light with residence where
        he has it all
            all of it.

                        The law is the sun and stars
                        The wheels turn at his bidding
                        In his hand
                        the voyage. And he knows it

Indifferent as the sea he walks above
his will with or against it, as
winds decide, or what god prevails.
His walk upon the bridge is its
        own ease and slope.
The movements are simple, watchful.
        No hunter   /   a sailor
his need for no man's love, not today.

                    Economy
is one occupation of the undiluted mind.

20 hours to midnight
      the mate's watch.

  He takes it clear of the net,
naming all the islands in the dark.
And when the islands slip behind us
      he names stars.

  Two changes of course :
he plots the third and draws, one side of the log
    painfully, a sketch of the ship :
        4 holds,
    the weight in each hold.
      Painful exactitude.
The Captain's will, the source of his extension.
    Inside his stubby body
                He writhes against it.
                But his love of number
                is arabic, and tender.

His core is a brutal resentment
    already balanced.
Softness in his movement, not command,
    hardly to be commanded,
    mastered still, but
              although he waits
              and hates, the
balance is laughter and love

even if the laughter is mocking

even if the loving is brutal.

      But he waits

and when the cat prowls the deck
  thin and alone,
it is he who bends to it, in a
  tenderness of recognition,
        how
  he himself moves.

       The ARSIA, *Split-Piombino*
       August 1955

1

Even in Algeciras
that cesspool :

when the wind came up suddenly
                    on a hot afternoon,

a half-dozen people on that corner
scrambled
          to pick up
                    gently
the empty cones of the ice-cream vendor
the gust had scattered .

2

Tonite,
after 10 minutes watching
and listening to early roosters
a dog joining in from the street
                    a lonesome ass
screaming from the market
for company
or food
          one
                    burst toward the Spanish coast
                    It was orange

Wires in the countryside are never still   :
between each pole they rise, dreaming upward
till each pole breaks their dream
and snaps them rudely back again to earth.
       Rise and fall.
       Rise, snap down and rise dreaming
against the early sky   patterns of wires
change their spatial relationships
parallel shifting lines streaming
crossing down the sky contract and open

Riding french trains
even italian trains,
you notice the wires beside the track
         rise and fall.
   In Spain
   if things are dull
you talk with people in the compartment.

   If the landscape is anything
   you cannot take your eyes off it.

Here are   3   mules threshing wheat
by running around in a circle
         dragging a sledge

There are   7   men asleep
under the tree at a station
        where we do not stop

There are adelfas blooming
wherever there is water,
following the lines of water
                    their fall of red

There is the head of a goat
showing above the embankment;
in his eye a devil
                    or some god

                    There is always something
to touch or feel or smell or see or people, you

never notice the wires.

All e v i d e n c e
of b i r d s i s q u e e r, the

square (it is not
square, inter-
section of 9th & 10th Streets, Second Avenue, near

   (and within the grounds)
   of a church called St. Mark's in-the-Bouwerie

(it is off the Bowery
at least a block off the Bowery) Bouwerie = farmland
and in this case, the Pieter Stuyvesant Farm, well, this
square
   is
   filled
   with . young . trees
   which in this case on

a minus-20 morning in February, are filled
      with sparrows
      screaming
as tho this snow were a spring rain somehow

   Another day (same month) another
   occurrence is clearer : off the Battery
against an ice-blue sky some gulls
so soundlessly, the
sound of their wings is all, they
   glide above the backs of boats, stern,
   up, crying, or surrealistically quiet .

And   .

in the body and wings of each bird   .   are   .

                    go—

SUMMER CLOUDS   /   HIGH AND
SWIFT   AGAINST   THE   HORIZON

                                or else the snow   .

THE ONE-NIGHT STAND :
an approach to the bridge

Migod, a picture window
both of us sitting there
on the too-narrow couch
variously unclothed
watching sky lighten over the city

You compile your list of noes
it is incomplete
I add another
there is no anger
we keep it open
trying,
shying
away, your all
too-solid body melts, revives, stif-
fens, clears and dis-
solves, an i-
dentity emerges, disappears, it is
like watching a film, the takes dis-
solving into other takes,
spliced suddenly to a closeup
The window tints pink
                              I wait
We sleep a bit   .   Your
identity goes and comes
it is never for me, it
is never sure of itself
                              I wait, you

ask too much of yourself, why
of the moment, why
is your fear of feeding off other people? Must
you always feed off yourself
and find it unreal food you eat, unreal
water you drink from the source of yourself, unreal liquor you take from the hand of a friend, and
never grow gloriously drunk, but stay
eating yourself
finding the fare thin,
stay in a dark room holding
uneasily, in an unreal hand
a thin man's unreal cock who stays
and grows more unreal to himself?

                              We both sleep.

New day's sun
doubles itself in the river
A double string of blue lights
glares to mark the bridge, the
city huddles under a yellow light
the sodium flares
gleam under oblique
sun's double in the stream,

                              I wake

ready, make my move.
"You'll make me pregnant" you murmur
and barely audible, "I'll die"
neither will stop me
your legs are open
I am there at the wet edge
of life, the moist living lips

It will not do
I have been at this life's edge
and hurt too many hours
It will be all me for a moment
then all you
Identities will dissolve
under this new act, or
six quick strokes
you move once
toward me, say
one word, even
moan, I will be finished
done
dissolved
become real, alone, no
it will not do
You are no victim and
I no rapist hero, I can
still, I
stop at the life's edge

Later
we are too real
separate, try
to recover
dully, our-
selves gone out
The coffee does not warm
there is an orange sun in the river
there are blue lights on the bridge
Animal tenderness and
sadness is all we salvage, is
all the picture window
mirrors and maintains

AN ATMOSPHERE,

                            or how
put it to you, render.

Tender is the.

Past has some dignity after all,
that is its re-al   —   its
                    virtue, that you
hold it close, hold it
CLOSE, whatever. I give you
you gave it first   .   It's

not hard to celebrate the sky
But I heard the bus come thru the block, the
bus after your bus, come
thru.
Two cats yowled, the starfish
held out its five arms

Aside,
that you wd not come to me
that neither of us can, nor want to
share the other, nor can we help it,
I wd not come to you, either, nor
need I have
The gin and tonic begun or never drunk, I
shall sit here with my red wine and mull
I shall mull my red wine and think
I shall think
red gin . mulltonic . sitwine
red mullet, ginthink, miltown, drink
the atonic mulled red, bink, bink,
bink, bink, bink. . . .

Out of the back window
from the wash hung two storeys up
water drops fall in the sun

slant past my floor on the light breeze
The filthy trees in my mind are never chopped down
are hung with bells tinkle in the light wind

in the light   From sunlight,
lowering the bucket into the deep well
hauled up again, tackle creaking, filled

with clear, cold
some water always slops from the zinc rim back
down, hear

waterdrops fall thru the blackness, scream,
splat, slop from the bucket, fuck it,
lift in both hands and drink

guzzling, holding the asses of young girls in our hands
drinking it all in, coffee or cream or both,
both sweet remembrance of

making it   .   not a thing on our minds
The silly-assed hard-drinking nights of our youth
and just making it to the bathroom in time

with shits the next morning,
warm shit leaking from our cracks .
15 years later we still talk . all night . The day

the black cat sits in the front window looking
out of our minds
down into the street with glazed eyes

screaming
at intervals
about her cunt-hole by Geoffrey,

letting the males know where she is
wanting to be where the boys are
or at least down in front of McSorley's

huddled, accepting their courtship,
watching the flies buzz
and the dog trot sidling past on a leash

interested,
not a thought on his mind,
but that eager innocent curiosity leaking

out of his muzzle, his ears, his musculature as he moves
past the cats
preparing to copulate

not a thought on their minds, sheer
intention, passive, passion, action
CAMERA, yellow filter for bright sunlight, their eyes

glaze .
They ignore him

NIGHT SITS
on the hawk's eyelid
                    mid-spring,
the tulips rejoice, the beds cannot keep from
blossom, nor from the fall of blossom, petals choosing dark
earth beneath all that bedding down who will lie on it

so to sleep, perchance   .
TO BLOSSOM, you damned perennial, up!
                    Tubes,
                    tubers,
                    bulbs,
                    carrots,
                    parsnips even, those leafy fields

Now spread, woman, right,
here we are, night,
the field of park, there the
moon is quarter-full
                    also a small cloud
                    and a star   .
                    And a star

PECK SLIP   .   smell of wholesale coffee
          floating in from Beekman, fish, a
wail of improbable proportions, tug
                    on the East River   .
       Bar is called THE PARIS   .   BELL & CO.,
          RING FISH, the
ring on my finger, my
toes parched on the stones.

Bells and whistles from the river.
The gulls circle and ride the wind above the bridge.
                    One
          rides it as slowly as possible,
          the line of his wings, leading-edge up
                    folding against it
               not soaring, no
          ecstasy, that hold, so
slow he moves in the glide, tension of wing strut,
          those bones
holding suddenly, suddenly

     doing a   b a r r e l   r o l l   not losing altitude   .
the control   .

at Park Place
or Dean Street
    across
decaying open platforms with their whitened wood
                  wash
waves of weathered greenness down the line
waves of somewhere unimaginable blossoms blowing
a late spring to tired faces   in this half-
    forgotten slow   half-empty train
passing in the rain   in slow dreams of pleasure
                toward the spur's end where
vaguely in-
decisively   train and rain
come at the same
time
        to a measured
                  stop

I think it
is its
location—
between 40th & 42nd—
gives it its princely
quality, by contrast

At the top of the steps in the spring dusk
the sun gone behind
Crompton Velvet & Union Dime, the massive stone
grace of the Public Library at one's back, the
loungers of varying quality on the stone benches
and about one on the steps, across the stairs stretched out
like so many Etruscan statues, old bums, the youngmen, the
college girls with their long legs under short skirts, curled
there on the steps in the fading light   . and below one
the lawn stretching out dark-green velvet all the way to
the fountain near Sixth Avenue, one can almost hear
the sound of falling water between the red and green
light interstices of evening traffic, plash, and at
regular intervals on this edge of lawn, between the
flower beds running an equal length, three signs

   KEEP OFF   KEEP OFF   KEEP OFF

simple enough   .   The trees
in lines, doubled at the far sides, have sent
the spring sap up and leaves, the first-broken buds
and moves of green have startled the streetlamps as they
open and see the blood has started up in the dusk, and

there the small leaves are
tender as the legs of girls
opening equally to night and
warm air   .   The flower beds
splay and tighten the tulips
the hands of men from the Park Department have planted
there
in, patterns of triangles, white intersecting the pink and
further down, pink intersecting red isosceles
cut to the side with sun   .   The other bed,
being shade-side, shows only green, the spikes, with
green spikes rising will be flowers tomorrow, next week,
a few white blossoms al-
ready out some halfway down toward the avenue
where buildings rise their own flowers of light, the ugliness
hidden in the new dark   .   I stand

arms parallel to the lines of balustrades, forward, out
stretching as though I were dusk or stone, above the girls,
the men
as though my hands were those of the Park Department
men, pressing
bulbs into the dark earth months ago, fall of the year,
my stone hands warm with sun, wet and dark with earth, o-
pening, closing, like the flowers all that action will become
tonight for me, now, this evening moment of new leaves
and grass.

The lawn stretches out its moment of princely peace   .
From the bottom of the steps one
cannot see the bare spots on it, it
stretches out perfect to the eye   .
There are those signs   .   For the moment I am
that tired monarch, that prince after a long day's riding

78

out for birds or boar or stag   .   I move my legs
lazily
          twice, and stand
                         at the edge of the grass.

The hour before dawn
fog came in   .   Stayed all day   .
Ragged thin filter of sun, a lover's
            touch on bared skin   .
            Dock smell, oil, machinery
            smell of sea,
            pulse of city in thigh-vein,
sea-pulse distends the delicate vein in the temple,
throbbing above eyes still caked with night   .   The head
            sways
            bends in amphibious light
on the dangerous shoulders of the day.

            At dawn
            all places equal   :
Athens, Paris, Brighton Beach and Arizona.
            The trap.
            The bear
dies in the trap   :   Mercury too a thief,
the cat's walk lives   .   The difference
            is feet

Feet   !   The cool air brushes an arm and
feet spring the walk, respond to the swaying head.
The sensitive pavement reacts, receives
holds the off-weight tread, holds and releases
wings to the god's foot man's foot, sends
an alternating current of love and sense
            between man and street.

Pay down the price of cigarettes, receive the pack, grasp
in the living hand, the cellophaned firmness   .   Dammit
          enjoy your smoke.
The sidewalks of spring
love us as we love them, no better, caress the feet
the way the feet press them   .   And sun, fog-
filtered, touches like lover   lovers' arms
who thieve each other   naked   tall   and warm.

The black-haired girl
with the big
        brown
                eyes
on the Queen's train coming
        in to work, so
opens her mouth so beautifully
        wide
                in a ya-aawn, that
two stops after she has left the train
I have only to think of her   and I
                        o-oh-aaaww-hm
                  wow !

Clickety-Clack

for Lawrence Ferlinghetti

I took
    a coney island of the mind
to the coney
island of the flesh
    the brighton local
    riding
past church avenue, beverly, cortelyou, past
    avenues   h & j
king's highway, neck road, sheepshead bay,
brighton, all the way to stillwell
avenue
    that hotbed of assignation
clickety-clack

I had started reading when I got on
and somewhere down past newkirk reached
number   29   and read aloud

                        The crowd
in the train
looked startled at first but settled down
to enjoy the bit even if they did think I
was insane or something
and when I reached the line   :   "the cock
of flesh at last cries out and has his glory

                        moment God"
some girl sitting opposite me with golden hair
fresh from the bottle began to stare dis-
approvingly and wiggle as tho she had ants
somewhere where it counted

                                    And sorry to say
5   lines later the poem finished   and I
started to laugh like hell   Aware
of the dirty look I was getting I
stared back at her thighs imagining
what she had inside those toreador pants besides
                           her bathing suit and, well
                        we both got off at stillwell

Watching her high backside sway and swish down that
street of tattoo artists, franks   12   inches long, past
                        the wax museum and a soft
drink stand   with its white inside,
I stepped beside her and said: "Let's
fling that old garment of repentance, baby!"
                                    smitten, I
hadn't noticed her   2   brothers were behind me

                        clickety-clack
                        Horseman, pass by

The loneliness
of a single coated figure in the rain,
the well-cut coat, the
face away for then
                          but there to
enter the glassed counter and order breakfast?
to know that inwardness of rain,
or that other
small lost face at the turnstile?
                          Impossible.
                          Done.

Magic of morning
walking thru the autumn of West 24th St. slowly
late to work
a schoolboy slowness along the sunburst sidewalk
Cold air, sun on the walls
one

sees
on the walk the broken bits
of color glistening in sun like frozen
smashed Christmastree decorations or bits of glass
imbedded in cement, that are only paper somehow, only
paper   .   No

sooner is that reality complete
ly absorbed, than another real thing rears its
multilimned head in the semblance of barrels, barrels
rolled past
dollies loaded with reams of printed sheets for the binder,
a reminder of work, the mist full of sun, the
barrels with bindings of bent under steam split willow
instead of
steel
tape binding, holding
china from England, to
feel filling the eye:
docks, warehouses, ship's hold, long-
shoremen, the wood
shavings and
the hands that wrought these, touched and shoved these
barrels
not

those that bought their transit, raked the profit in,
               but a cooper's dream of death
                    these broken staves
singing themselves in the last triumphant crackling song
                              of fire
the barrels being burnt
unUSE again,   U N U S E   .   The

park is still green but leaves have fallen already, some
raked in piles and miles of countryside stretch out
                         filling the eye   :
heaped leaves burning at roadside, the air blue
                    acrid   .   Nostrils
sting with the smoke of years we no longer remember
                    except with the rare
          attack of the senses   .   Still,
the tender drooping spray from the fountain
center of park, has old dixie cups, tops from
icecream cartons, burnt matches and other rubbish to be
                              its birds
                              and its fish

Move along
move along
don't care
cold air, the
sun, the sun   .   I
wish I were far from here

O,   t o   l o o k   at all those revolutionaries,
Siqueiros, en seguida, and all that, sed
Muntanyer
            I'm her Grendel,
            she's my
d a m n , if I have to stay here with my images,
we are still all glad we have met again   . Large smiles   .

I have met two old friends in the bright sunlight
& to come at last to that
Gate 4, Section 11., November 28 and a long dream &
I cannot find my way from one long street to the other, or
the through streets do   n o t   run thru, and the vowels
make it
so long   :
            Dear Labyrinth, o double-bitted axe, o friend,
            you are swinging, and how sharp you are, you
keep turning, and it doesn't matter which way, or
art thou still sometimes, or still, as they say, twisting?
I still haven't got to the end of you,,,,,,,, I shall
never catch up, but
                        still glad to see you!
                                Large smiles.

                    A fly
                 sits &
scrubs his front feet,
the rubs his back feet together

                              cleaning them, then
washes his wings and his eye   .   Why
do people call flies dirty?

It looks like a pleasant process   .

Self-absorbed & self-contained,
directed, especially in flight,
certainly curious and active—

W h y   i s   b u z z i n g   c o n s i d e r e d   i d l e ?

Two blocks away
night traffic goes whipping through
the avenue,
the fast motors.

It's not as tho one could see it
It's not as tho nothing were good

Even above the rooftops stars are mixed with cloud
only the brightest come through:
the absolute bureaucracy of size and closeness
which coefficient is power.

But the cat
crosses the tiled roof at this hour
in the dark night
in the moon.

Málaga, September 1956

Montalban, Nᵒ 3, piso 2ᵒ

                          is not exactly a pension

but a lady who rents rooms

                    occasionally.

      And this big room has a small sink

      with a tap where

      no water has ever run:

                    and a drain

      in which one sets a cork.

      And on the brass plate is written

           VERDAGUER   BARCELONA

that half-mad priest and poet

who listed all the peaks

in the catalunyan Pyrenees,

and here you are on a sink-drain.

Has it come to this, Jacint?

    Also

there are two balconies looking out

over the roofs of the city

                  to the mountains.

And the lady, when she was younger,

                  lived in Granada

and remembers that Garcia Lorca

always wore broad-brimmed Córdoban hats

        and a black string-tie, and was

                un chico simpático.

So
it is not very strange
that the words are always there
when one looks out of the window
over the roofs of the city

"and to see clouds and mountains
in the motionless distances
the heart twists in itself"

"y al mirar nubes y montes
en las yertas lejanías
se quiebra su corazón
de azúcar y yerbaluisa"

Why do gulls like
to sit in the sea
only when there are waves, when
there is ground swell?
And never will
when it is smooth?
Must be they take pleasure from
the motion of wave
as I do,
the lift and ride and rise, the swing
down the trough, climbing
effortlessly
the next crest.

Best to sit in the sun afterward, tho,
on rock,
watching the rollers break, spill-
slide up the beach,
letting spray fall back its jet
upon wet rocks, brown legs, the next
against the sun.
We never learn
to distrust such motion, Carroll.

I recall your long legs
tumbling in such a sea
at Bañalbufar that summer,
white
body reddening
taking its first day's sun
with brown face set on top with already
thinning hair.

93

Caring, steadily caring, for ideas alone
had not kept you from trying to rise
to your feet, smiling against such a sea,
the surf cracking you back to a sitting
                    posture against the stone
beach, the sea sliding around you
no god to help you, only your stalk-
                    white, reddening legs
could lift you timed in the face of it.
No god there that afternoon, Carroll,
only our powers, not yours, our demons
sea   .   sun   .   wind-squall
                    among us found a balance.
It was your own.

                    This winter sun
        streams across my legs and chest, flashes
            across the crashing surf-line.
A fisherman comes down with a heavy line and
drags it out its length along the beach,
                        heaving
                        each portion out
                        into the surf
until it's a snake part in, part out of water.
        He washes, not too carefully
            the oil slick off it   .   Long rope
it takes him a long time   .   He finishes finally
and sticking to rock
avoiding the sand he
hauls it again to the top of the sea-
                wall and coils his rope
                    to dry in the sun,
slows his coiling to talk to a friend
                    gives the line at last turn
                        the work done.

When will we learn
so naturally to
quit, when what we have to do
                    is done?
        Or that the print of rough stone,
                        rock
set deep in the flesh of the palm,
            my own or yours,
see what we will in reading it, patterned
        palms   .   pyramids   .   cuneiform
                tablets, a cross, some
small starched waves or winging gulls, the shell,
                the flower
        we see or think we see   .   there
no matter
we trust and fear
this movement, that god,
                will disappear
                        inside this quarter-hour?

                    Málaga, Winter 1956-57

Monday morning early
Sunday evening late

A tram goes by, outbound
taking the late drinkers
the restless moviegoers
or the blossoms of girls with their escorts
home
      sleep

The conductor on the final run
standing there in his slippers
      facing the track

The ladies sit at café tables in twos
An old man sits
      reading at a table alone

      the new day's news
letting his beer get warm
letting the sky be enough

Málaga, Winter 1956-57

It saves the city
a provincial other
wise port, how the bloody
ships come in, the sheer
machinery of docking, un-

                (how we knock the other larger
             ports to the north, Cádiz & Huelva to the
             west

loading certain hatches
creak of crane, the strain of ropes, the rub of hulls,
that close smell of sea-rotted wood

and the wine inshore in bars we'll come to later, not
any dream of release but real
                      cold
                        and flowing
release we cannot beg or steal, but come to later
nub of skulls on hillsides, sweating bodies, gypsies
under the bridge on beds of caña, closed? open mouths
                            of bitches
dull strain of guitars below, the bold song rising, the hips
rising and the swing of the bloody knockers
steers the world back home .

Que buen
> *números me quedan!*

Mañana
> luck is
> always for tomorrow
> or tonight, when
the lottery is drawn

The horse-drawn carriage rattles
and clatters down the street
The horse's bells jingle
on the embroidered harness
The driver sits alert and wears
> a hat
> That is part of it

No one pays attention
The man will pay the driver
The cobbles will stay in the street
> but luck is felt
in the small dark stores, the doorways
as the sound of bells and hoofs
on cobbles

Travelers are good luck
here
they cry *"maleta! maleta!"*
and run and touch the suitcase
> for luck

"   Nail
those long shadows to my cross   !
darkened doorways in sun-glare
a hammer
                Silence of black skirts
                unbelted
In the shadowed eyes
an ultimate patience
Death lives among the people
                as Life does

Luck never
Luck is for people in carriages
                for voyagers

Que buen números me quedaan
                        para H O Y!
            último par' H O Y!

N⁰ 000549

Loteria Nacional

Sorteo
15 de Enero de 1957
=

El Portador
interesa 1 peseta al
número

59.174

Today makes   20   days
that some ants follow the same route
                across   2   of these steps
                never varying from the line.
Always this same line of ants
across the same   2   steps   .
They may even be the same ants,
tho this would make a difference   :
if the line budged one centimeter
                it would make a difference.

And I do not know what the job is
or when it will be finished.

White snow of paper sugar
wrappers on the floor
next the counter.
2   men stand over their wine
                                        (white)

The men are white
The wine is white
                        Two
women come in, they order hot

milk   .   Everything is still white
                                        (white)

Finally someone orders a cake
                        I pluck
        courage up
        and order
                        black
                        coffee
                                        (black)

Málaga, Winter 1956-57

Before the cathedral, the plaza
is a forest
                        tall fronds
The trunks are people in bright clothing
the plaza in bright sunligh⸍
the yellow palm leaves waving

            young forest on a brilliant breeze
            in the bright air of heaven.

                        At no signal
                  the trees face the church
        and stamp with the butt of the fronds
                              muffled sounds
                  but in unison.   Aediles
        demanding for the whole people, a benison
                              which is given.

Afterwards,
the children carry them mostly,
slowly through the streets of the city,
walking home from the mass.

        "Mine is taller'n yours!"
        —*El mio es mas alto qu'el tuyo!*
        —*No es verdad! Mira! Mira!*

Whipped to competition, the palms wave unconcernedly
            in the bright air

102

in the shadows.
                    Pigeons walk in the sunlight.
                    The people feed them.

                    ❋

Death day by the sea without crosses. The beach
stretches its cold sands under
a dirty sky full of scud. The wind
chill.
No trees, nothing to break it.
All the tears have fallen already into the sea.
Even the sourness of salt on the air is galling,
the surf   dull and lifeless   but continuing.

Clouds darken on the horizon at three o'clock.
The wind picks up.

                    ❋

          The ark of the tabernacles
          is drawn by two white bullocks
          with olive-branch tied to their horns.

They stand white and imperturbable
among the fireworks.

                    Barcelona   .   Sète   .   Firenze
                    Holy Week   .   1956

You can have it by being in it
you can have it by dancing and drinking
you can have it by being jostled by crowds
                or standing in the street yelling
             or standing and listening quietly   :
                but in words it is not possible
to have it.

             There were

                        fires in all the streets
             at every intersection, bonfires,
             noise all night in the streets
                        in the parks
             carnivals
                  & fireworks.

Dancing all the next afternoon
in the Plaza de San Jaime,
the bodies weaving like wheat
a whole plaza-full of movement   :
and when the music rises, comes
      down harder on the beat at
the end of the *coblas,* a whole sea
leaping circling saulting bodies, the
      waves of the sea.

      Go ahead, lieutenant, photograph it.

                        In the Junta del Puerto
                  2 streets blocked off for dancing.
Not the delicate & precise steps of the *sardanas*
      in the Plaza, the ordered circles,

circles within circles, here
the individual abandon of couples
the individual shyness of couples
   and the music from loudspeakers
   and boys walking off to the beach with their girls.
                Fiesta.
                Potato chips and *churros.*

                Impossible, impossible,
the life's too near the skin—now look,
   in the Junta del Puerto, fires.
They drink beer from the glass *porones,*
2 streets blocked off by dancers, the music
audible from the shore, surf juxtaposing.
                Bars
                       open all nite,
                fires throughout the city.
The clack of the watchman's stick,
the formal and delicate dancing.

                In the calle de los Marineros
                a small girl in a white dress
                a small boy with a firecracker.

                                    Barcelona
                            23-24 de junio 1955

At seven in the summer evenings
they crowd the small stone benches
back to back
five and six to a bench;
young mothers
old men
workers on their way home stopping
off, their faces
poised in the tiredness and blankness
recouping
taking the evening coolness
five and six to a bench.
Children too young to walk,
on the knees of their mothers
                              make
seven and eight to a bench.

                    The older ones play immies
                       or chase each other
                          or pigeons.

Sun catches the roofs, one side
                         of the arcade;
the whole of the plaza in shadow between
seven and eight of an evening.

                    The man with balloons
                    rises above it almost
                    his face deflated & quiet
                                        blank

106

emptied of the city
as the city is emptied of air.
The strings wrapped to his hand
go up and do not move.
He stands at the edge of the square
not calling or watching at all.
                                    The cart
with candy has food for the pigeons . . .

                                        A lull,
        a lull in the moving,
        a bay in the sea of this city
                into which drift
five and six to a bench
seven and eight to a bench

                Now
                the air moves the palmtrees,
                faces.
                All of it gentle

                Barcelona . 27 . VI . 55

A goat lies in the grass beside
      a dry irrigation ditch

        Sun-glitter on sea
The boats drift in with the tide

Grazing cattle shy away
their long horns down & waving
In the hills the earth is red
      What a day!

Along the road, a gypsy
raises her water gourd
      in a fine
gesture to the passing bus

"QUIERES?"
            "PROVECHE!"

                      Málaga-Algeciras
                      November 1956

political poem I :
THE POLITICIAN'S SWEETHEART

has just turned 22,
reclines on those soft cushions with her drink
and couldn't care less where the nearest
deep shelter is located, those cushions;
luckily,
she does not care much for politics.

And Art?
A Debussy tone poem, she often says,
is that an answer to anything?
It's those cushions under her ass.
They respond to her velvet pressures.
It's a different world.
The brass, then the percussion.

My teeth are metal in my mouth
clash, taste of cash, quarters,
Kennedy half-dollars   .   Growth
average of   10   choice stocks
into which set

        feet

        hands

        wrists, that otherwise
might move, live   .   Right,

           on rights
the north is as the south, my
teeth are metal in my mouth   .

YOUR LOVE like any cage
    I say, has bars
that break my head, my pride, my balls
besides all which is wet but not
    hot somehow.

Well.
There is moisture I am thinking of, a rain
    which is not gold
cometh not from the father,
silver rain of the moon, a softness
I trust in,
as well as an implacability
feminine and effulgent.
I think about this when I am alone
              or
"it is so goddamned dry on these rocks"

Seeds on my desk
rotate, take root before me, my
mind dreaming controls
"the nature of plants, bodies, etc."
"How bud we our way into spring
combined bringer of forsythia?
                    (soil)
                    crocus the locus,
cloak us in blue skies
fuck us in sunlight
rook us in birdflight north
invoke odd gods, on the brownstone stoops
            joke with broads in the sunlight
            poke at the railings, flowers & branches
make
old women jealous, old men
sick to their stomach, failing
to join the season
                    give back
what winter took," she sed,
& disappeared into the bushes   .

It falls.
The night falls
the night sky falls
a star, the eyes follow, my
hand falls
It is never enough   /   I
am hardly ever enough
even to myself

I go.
I go through the streets
I cross avenues, helpless against your anger
I go pulverized through narrow streets with paving stones
Let the walls fall, crumble, fall, crush me finally, end it
                        the eyes   /   the hands
Your cunt is tight with anger
I can feel it a block away, your
                        belly is tight
your asshole is loose with disdain
and fear

And I cannot stand it, your beauty
walks beside me like a
tree in motion under the wind
of my desires, with
standing them   /   standing in
an emptiness not your own that you hate
and feel it is your own   .   It is not, it
is mine also, let me, that damned sea,
I will come

It falls.
The half-hour would-be wholeness
falls, the year falls, the mirror
destroys itself   /   that year, a
brilliant, at times quiescent
star will fall
into the sea
I will come

I lie down   /
the trees are bright with resisting
polished under the rain   .   have shed all their leaves
                    Corridors
of summer stretch out behind me endless
                    like memory like
I destroy myself running through open doors
leading through empty rooms
Or there is someone
huddled in a corner
                    pissing   /   Yes.
I humiliate my life, piss it away, I am
my shoes, my black pair of sneakers walking
corridors, deserted beaches, cement sidewalks, sit
now beneath a chair   .   torn   .   quiescent   .   my
laces flopped sideways on the floor
                    fit, however,
to the foot, dingy shape of life
smelling of dried sweat, revived
                    at any warmth
my worn fabric
yes, the corrugations

                    I shall come
shaping all truths from my own balls, seeking in my skull

even those shaped years ago   /   I was too young, I looked
for a shadow at ten in the morning which will not appear
until four in the afternoon   /   my own
with the sun from the other direction and
                              everything failing

I will come, I
shall come into your body as into the morning world,
as into a city filled with its leisure and softness,
where the soft light falls on the bird, the tree, the wall,
where the sun of mid-day is lost on the shadows of palm trees
                              arcades
                        Fountains cool it
I shall come through your eyes from the other side, my
                        water, my mirror
I will come into your belly and make it a sea rolling against
                                                    me,
come into you soft as sleep   /   and be real

                        You will cry the whole afternoon

A gust of wind blows papers in the parking lot like leaves
Then rain comes at the window
My girl comes at the door, my
desk and floor are littered with papers   When
                              we kiss the sheets of paper
move gently

fish nibble at the surface
also down below   .
my love and i spend less time so
than we would wish

belly to belly fast
and sometimes slow,
fish nibble at the surface
also down below

rooms not our own
we make our own and go
belly to belly fast
and sometimes slow   .

gulls are our birds and dive
the dove, the sparrow
also prove our heat and beat
against the wings of rooms we fill and leave

hands that walk and move
or wave and slow—
our hands have fasted
more than we would wish

the winter beach
will be half-filled with snow
unlike the summered spring
we reached the crest

of that spring tide i sing
clutched to one another thru
the forests of the bmt, the slow
reaches of the brighton line, to

break the fast of hands
we go and go, and
come at last to that
whipped all over with sunlight
sea   .

Windows are
steps of light
running down into darkness
From the lowest yellow step
one falls into backyard blackness

The upper one near the roof steps off
into dark glow of sky
the immense black rose of the city
curbing the eye

Lamplight falls one
corner of the bed
Sliding off the pillow   her bright sleeping
head fashions shadow low on the shoulder
her curled white body hugs
the afternoon's sprung seed

The Proposition

After she
had complained about
men

nearly a solid hour
to her friend's mother
she

was visiting her friend
and her friend's mother
in the country, her

girlfriend left the house
to look for the cat
and she

continued the re-
petitive argument which
her friend's mother

listened to patiently
without comment
until (while)

her daughter was gone
out, (looking for
the cat)

and she said for the
hundredth time how really
awful bastards

men were, and didn't she
(the mother) think there
WAS

something else to be in-
terested in, or
wasn't it

time to try something
new, the mother
after long silence

said: "I. wouldn't
be new
to me, but I'm

ready anytime you are."
The girlfriend
returning (with the cat)

was a trifle con-
fused when her friend in-
sisted she had to catch the late bus home (there

was some editing she
HAD to do). "I hope she wasn't
offended, or anything,"

the mother, after having
driven the girl to her bus
explained

to her daughter, on
the way home the very
probable reason her

friend had left to
go back to the city
so sudden-like

Flocculations of cirrus hang
                              precipitate
in the tube of sky above the street,
roof the eye aging in its pool,
                              enclosing its
own reflection with a crust of ice
                              Crack
Dull, but
the eye looks out
and lines of random sheep grazing above the park feed
on the only grass there is this winter morning
                    /
                         in the mind
The eye, yes
                    aging in its pool,
but open   .

O P E N

Upon returning home tonite
and it is a home
now
surely,
being the animal I am
when I had undressed, I
wrapped my hand around my
balls, and their now-limp appendage.
And afterward
smelled my hand.

It was you.
As your perfume is still on my undershirt
so this perfume also.

Dried green leaf on the door
Blackened leaf below it

      Under that a metal leaf, blackened also
      Below that the leafy ace of clubs

Outside the window the tree I thought a friend
has undressed all its branches & is ugly to me

Returning home defenseless
even a stray dog barked at me
I could not even declare my love to him
much less my innocence.   Branches
of frozen breath writhed from both our mouths
          into the air

      Even the room is cold
      & here I sit and stare
      & barely move

SUBWAY STOP at Wall Street,
    the girls
    going to work at
    ten of nine
    are so much prettier
    than those walking out
    at 9:30

Tho, occasionally at 10,
you see a beautiful woman.

It is time to be silent.
It is time to be that tower that
in this woman, a child

           lusts for.

It is good to know someone
who does not confuse this
possibility, this
meeting in the forked young branch of eternity

        (its own purity, its
         own tree)

             with love.

The girl with the beautiful legs
walks down a Brooklyn street
a hope-and-a-half away

Terrible indeed is the house of heaven in the mind
soft
giving back the quiver
deeper and deeper disclosed until the blind
sun bursts
into a close warm black behind the eyes
                              yellow stars
                              then the red

Light perspiration on bodies engraved as beads
                              upon the stone mind
the heavy, delicate odor, the swift
calling by name, the pronouns
the arching back
a sky under which the blood speaks
its flood
                              its ebb
what the man must do
what the woman must

AND LOVE
has gone else
where, my mind, gloved and shot
even the hall is dark as
I glot toward bed

It is not
I do not love
you, dear, we
are both elsewhere   .

the rivers of afternoon
flowing about you as you
move   . stop, standing
afterward in my bathroom
naked among the young plants
in the green light singing
softly to yourself

O, Danny Lynch be sittin below there in McSorley's
having an India Pale & a porter & a bit o' conver-
sation & I
not joinin him, what whith his black eye an' all   .

        Instead,
        I come direct up to bed,
        wheer the wife do be readin the newspaper
        & don't even move over for me   .

I understand what the solution is, but
what be the question   ?

He t'ought it were a weddin but
it was a funeral   .   So?
        what is the question   .   or,
        who is a friend of the groom   ?

Friday night
free night
night of
Freya, up-
on the town

After the night out
                    (on the town) after
an overbibulation
dedicated alternately
to good & evil spirits,
it is all soft   .
                    "Fuzzy," she thinks,
          pro-pretero-nymph she is become
          climbing these stairs, turns
upon the stairs, smiling
at him, at the top of her
stairs

          No flight upon the hills
                    from the thyrsus he
carry before him, overcoming all, in-
cluding
her anticipation
                    "Would you like
                    coffee?" she
          smiles, turning upon the stairs   .   His
head comes up to the level of the
stanchion formed by the innominate bones
                    of the ilium

the "mixed inflorescence" where
"the primary ramification is centripetal (or indeterminate,
& the secondary & successive ramifications
are centrifugal
& determinate"
                    She smiles at the
                                top of the stairs
Vine and ivy branches twine up about
the thyrsus of Dionysus,
pinecone tip on the staff, thud
of blood under his thumbnail in the
hand that holds open & unpapered, a
            spray of lilac, a burst of mixed
            inflorescence already moving toward
                    secondary ramifications, he
                    also smiles,
                    his head at the softened (△) delta
"Yes," he says, and raising his eyes finally,
        "that would be very nice. Thank you."

How the lines run down into the night
a forest of trees standing up
It is a park
                    / mise-
          rere nobis   ,   4 voices on the
Adoremus te   .   Orlandus Lassus (1532-94)
they are
a quarter-of-a-tone
off, my friend says   .   They
                    fuck it up
                    Don't we all   .
Give the child words, give him
words, he will use them   .   give
him words
                    / Have
(miserere nobis)
mercy on us.

How the trees hang down from the sky
grey winter down, in violet light
how the city rises about us, in the
dusk, drinking us in   .

Each day I open the cupboard
& the green shoots of my last onion
have in the dark grown higher

   A perverse & fairly final pleasure
that I love to watch him stretching himself
secretly, green sprouting shamelessly in
this winter, making a park in my kitchen, making
spring for a moment in my kitchen

that, instead of eating him
   I have watched him grow

"Do you fuck on a first date?"
       I asked her, as we left the church,
ashes on both our foreheads. "No,
but I gobble good as a
young head ought to," she sed
      which is cool,
which is better than Madisonavenueing it
should anyone ask .

or a raisin in the sun.

   3 small boys
   taking 2 steps
   down at a time clatter on the
   sidewalk in front.
   The big thumbmarks
   make them look
   like some secret organization.

"You got the dice?" one asks
another, the head shrug once, "No,
Joey's gott'em." Ah,
there's nuthin' like a
little penance on a nice day
to set a sinner up!

The sun comes and
                   comes
The buildings against the sky
yellowed stone, red brick, against the blue
bright metals against the blue
                   Today and yesterday
our first two days of winter are two words
          gray/blue   rain/sun   Sun
comes and goes and comes against the brick walls
across the street, the stained green cornices, the white rags,
clouds move. Shadows sharpen and fade
Sound of roller skates, bicycle bells, children's
                   voices in the street
A telephone rings somewhere.
No one answers it

                   words, no words.
The birds sail singly or in pairs, their
shadows move against the brick and disappear
          We are men and we have words
The shadow of a flock swings down across the building
and up, past the turn, the underwings catch light,
white as the rags
blue as the sky
grey as yesterday
                   The sun comes and comes
The young cat sits in my window
          black as hell

      The apartment
near emptied by now,
everything moved to 9th Street
but one basket of paperwork, one
lamp, eight books, some poems & a typewriter,
three near-empty bottles of booze, a chair, the desk
and—yes—the bed

      At breakfast coffee
      these last mornings,
I make her use the wooden chair,
I improvise a seat, a
yellow-painted old milk crate
with the Manhattan telephone directory dropped inside for
                                                    weight

      As she leaves for work
      this morning, she
stands in the doorway and laughs to see
me sitting over my last cup of coffee,
                        seedy
with a three-day beard & my morning hardon rising
absently against the short, red-and-white-trim black robe,
gift of my friend in Japan, sitting
                        seriously
on the yellow box crouched over the Scotsman Finlay's
                                                    poems
come from Kyoto yesterday, aloud, with the sun pouring in
on my left hand & the brick wall crowding back empty
away from the scene

She in her black-and-brown dress
& high heels leaving for the business world
with this rustic scene in her eye,
      laughs . Confusedly prolonging the impression
I do not even rise, she comes
                  to me to
                  have her good-
                  bye-kiss

Any mountain climber will tell you
it's a matter of knowing yourself,
your skill   .   Even the older men,
a world locked in itself, as also
the laws of place escape us, hem us in, in
some forgotten way, as themselves   :

"Am I ready for this mountain?"
and they go.   Up.

Around   6   of a summer evening
the pigeons are that engaged.
On the east front of the Public Library at 42nd Street
it is a matter of sitting.
On the wall SE of the entrance from 5th Avenue, seven or
eight

stand on a narrow ledge
and are falling asleep
or about to, beaks
turned to the wall, fall
asleep   .

Four on the south urn,
on the north urn three.

A third of the way up the face, on
the edge of the second ice-field, not
just the rain of pebbles and dirt, but
going flat on your face, falling rocks
flashing off hats, shoulders,

140

smashing plastic cups in the knapsacks,
the sheer face, the near misses . . .

             Standing on the north lion, one,
                    on the south lion, two pigeons.
On the rounded edge of the empty fountain, south
side of the steps, one lies down   . Not all those
against the wall seem asleep, even immobile, but most .

in some forgotten way
we carry the marks of places all our lives,
a kind of fate   .   her   .   whoever she is,
she swings on his arm and smiles, leans
        toward us
        and smiles .
I acknowledge the greeting somehow and
squeeze Sara's hand at the same time   .   This
world, the double avenue of trees, this
world is locked in itself, a central lawn,
the flower beds empty .

On this west side facing the park,
there are two birds who walk alone, circle
about one another,
puffing and circling slowly. The
game
is for the smaller one to seize the beak of the larger
and pull it down to the stone.
They grapple beaks and bob,
interminably almost. On
one corner of my bench a
girl in tight slacks is writing a long letter to a boyfriend.
She reads his letter over first, then begins her own:
"O God, I can't say it. If I only could" it starts. She also

watches the two pigeons at their beak game, hand across
her breast
resting on her shoulder while
she watches the beak game
and thinks of the next sentence.

A third of the way up, it's a way of knowing yourself, the
                                                            world
not locked in its place but all that mountain coming down
in pieces on the back, shoulders, I'm flat on my, the arm
covering the face, tick-tick, will I ever get off it? whack!
another rock hits the knapsack, get up and go on?

       The pigeons seem never to tire
       of the game.
       Do any of us?
       Finally they circle and stroll, drop
       down
               toward the lawn,
       stroll off into the sunset together
              sort of .
                             Ro-mance   .

or back down again?
Locked in myself   .   her   .   whoever she is   .
The way is focused,
the formality of a way into life,
twice, three times attempted   .

BRING a leaf to me
just a leaf just a
spring leaf, an
april leaf
just
      come

Blue sky
never mind
Spring rain
never mind
Reach up and
take a leaf and
      come
just come

Over the right
triangle formed
by Stuyvesant St. & Ninth, the
wellknit blonde in a blue knit dress &
the hair piled high

crosses on the hypotenuse, jiggles

t
w
o
w
o
r
l
d
s

& several hemispheres as she walks.

                              The trajectory
causes a mass cessation of work
at a Con Edison encampment on
one of the other two sides, all
orange equipment with dark red flashers, flags
at the corners of the encampment wave cheerfully

in the Monday morning breeze, all the orange helmets
facing the same way, eyes right, and clearly

everything else is right

Click
click

the heels go at an easy pace across Stuyvesant
touch the curb at Ninth, jiggle-jiggle   .   The
          e x p l a n a t i o n
is printed on the sides of all the equipment, even on one
                                        flag   :
          D I G   W E   M U S T

They dig   .

"Shultzie?"
                —Yeah.
"The game's over?"
                —Yeah.
"The Yankees lost?"
                —Yeah,
"Good—you got any melons up your house?"

> *See, see rider*
> *see what yu hev done*
>
> *See, see rider*
> *see what yu hev done*
>
> *Let me be yr side-track*
> *till yr main line comes*
>
> *O, careless love*

I. *It's Always You*

I realize
I shut my eyes
when we make it, baby

hoping that we
'll turn out to be
some other couple entirely

II. *Someone*

O, there is some dame I am longing to see
                    I know that she
                    'll turn out to be
                    someone
who'll climb over me   da da
                                        da da
                                        da da

III. *The A Train*

Shooba   .   doobe-do
you-shd-take-the-A-train
         sd Duke Ellington:
         "Evvabuddy knows whea Sugar Hill is"
that song was
properly,
writ without words

         Shoo.ba.doo.be.doo   /   Now try
the longing here for you, the very
                          very
                          thought of you
my love   .

IV. *You'll Never Know*

The light crazy beautiful heavy feeling in my
                          legs and arms
trying to run away
I'll come back someday
to somebody

But for now, baby, it's just wonderful
and
      all
            down
                  hill

V. *Before It's Too Late*

         I'm leaving town, baby
         and going to Bolivia
         to dig rin-tin-tin

148

Someone
who smells you there
at 5 A.M. in the yellow light.
Summer.
And I smell you, the places
where our bodies touch are warm, I
hear the small tune your breathing
makes no word, my head
   and shoulders move in the dawn to catch
      the different angles of some sleeping
face and flesh
where it takes
air beside me.

I take air, I
smell you
there beside me
in the yellow light, I catch
different angles of your face and breasts, the
hipbones jutting just
and sleek below soft belly, the
face is different each
time I move, the angle of hip, the rounding of

breast . At Guadalajara, 55
kilometers from Madrid
     all
       the advertisements say, I
rise on one elbow, scramble down, and
rest my head between your legs to

taste you, the
only thing
left.

Hands

Her room is
stuffy, she notices,
as they enter it

After fucking on the light,
as she thinks of it, throwing
the light sweater on a carefully madeup bed, she

moves quickly to the
window, he is close behind her, as
she bends to throw it up
he takes the crests of
        both ilia in
        his hands to
        press
her ass against, her crack against his . . .
        "Wait a minit, cancha
        wait a minit?"
she yells, bringing
one thing up, & another
down   .

Winding past
all those undulating
O NO, thighs, just to
get a couple of drinks?

        And the piano player with the group, the
        only whitey and the only
        one with an idea
        in his ear, and
        even that much too slick and
        even that should kick a long so-
        lo along

"There're a lot of funny fat ladies here tonite,"
Sara says .

That is true.

Imagine a young woman
lying on her back at the intersection
Third Ave. and 8th St., at Astor Place, no,
      not fallen, but on her back,
reclining there in the snow, looking
alive, up at the passing crowd, they
part afraid to look but those that do,
      the men,
she raises an amorous clouding of their eyes.

     It is a threshold I cross, no
     longer an intersection, the bird
hidden in the shirt upon the chest
torn   . the eye
swells in the head
bird flutters and falls into the sea of eyes
     She was so beautiful
Bird and sun are holy take the head
tear it open and set it like a
melon upon the threshold .
             I cross .   Everything
that lives, Blake says, is holy   .   yes
Bird, sun, eyes, the street, the intersection, the fish (hip) swims from between my legs,
LEAPS, yes, that was a year ago.
        But that silken trap.

Love drinks itself and is drunk.
The girl gets up off her back
and walks off quick, a clust-er

of sparrows bursts from the intersection into
                    grey sky .
The eyes around the bed I sleep in
                    watch   .   That silken trap
Fucking drunk   .   Over the cold shadow of the street
        running.
        After her.
Call it the net of lust   .

Impact of these splendid
       things
upon the appropriate sense
How refuse to meddle with it, throw it away, play
to hide our passion in the dance of that moon
      upon the small waves, how come to it hugely
      erected and keep, we tell ourselves, a just balance be-
tween the emotion and the motion of wave on the bay, the
leap of the dolphin in our dreams, accompanying us home?

Hello moon.

From the *Mary Murray*'s upper deck
the wind is stiff in our faces
               Another spring as warm
               10 days earlier
               the moon is still out
another year falling across its face so slowly, so flatly the motion of wave as I do
fall back astonished, take my glasses off, the shore lights
so close,
fuzz to myopic eyes sting in wind, the
tide is full, he said, the moon lies fair upon the straits.
Let me tell you, let me tell
you straight, strait and very narrow indeed, encloses

Lights white
or red mark the
bell buoy's
clang against the dark bay
over it, over   .   it   .   The tail

of a Brooklyn ferry disappears behind
an anchored tanker, fail,
I fail to see and put glasses back on,
I fail
to   .

Laughter along the lift of deck,
lovers stand at the rail, close on
From the rail we see
fire-glow from the interior of the
island, smoke-smell drifts out
across the lower
                    bay,

to us, ten days later, a year gone,
            burnt across a bright face
that looks like it's been chewed on,
                    but will not die   .

The quarter-moon glints on the water
            nailed, nailed on the sky

Goodbye moon   .

Red wine, half-a-bottle I had
found in the surf at Bridgehampton
in the afternoon
    COOL FROM THE SEA
Al tasted it with me   .

Evening   .   sundown   .
     mockup of the day   :

having slammed my left thumb in the car door

I cut myself on the can opener

     opening hot beer   .

God knows it might have happened to anyone.

Only
the beachday over, I
slipped on the steps of the ho-tel
    and had to
use my sprained right arm to catch
       with to
save the delicate joining membranes of
the carapace of deathshead monster horseshoe crab

I had found on the beach,

had saved from the day, the tide.